Love

I love you

HarperCollins*Entertainment*
An Imprint of HarperCollins*Publishers*
77–85 Fulham Palace Road,
Hammersmith, London W6 8JB

www.harpercollins.co.uk

Published by HarperCollins*Entertainment* 2004
5 7 9 8 6

A catalogue record for this book
is available from the British Library

ISBN-13   978-0-00-717846-9
ISBN-10   0-00-717846-8

Printed and bound in Italy by L.E.G.O. SpA

LOVE

You are like a wonderful LOVE CHOCOLATE – not one of the RUBBISH ones that nobody wants to eat but a REALLY NICE ONE that ALWAYS GOES FIRST !!

A LOVE CHOCOLATE

The LOVERS

Arm in arm they stand
on the SAUSAGE of LOVE
looking out together at the
KETCHUP of their DREAMS

Sometimes the HEART
should FOLLOW the MIND

Sometimes the HEART
should tell the MIND to
STAY AT HOME and
STOP INTERFERING

LOVE

This picture of my DREAM shows
how much I LOVE YOU*

* if you are not impressed by the biscuit thing PLEASE remember that it was only a DREAM

I LOVE you more than "THINGS"

Please understand that men have an **UNNATURAL PASSION** for non-living objects ("THINGS") so this is quite a **NICE** thing of me to say

Examples of "THINGS"

The POTATO of LOVE

It is so full of LOVE that the ANGELS weep with envy at its coming and the HEAVENS sing a NEW and BEAUTEOUS song

I LOVE you SO MUCH that every night I Shout out your BEAUTIFUL name to the distant STARS*

*until the nice men come to take me
away again

The SHAPES of LOVE

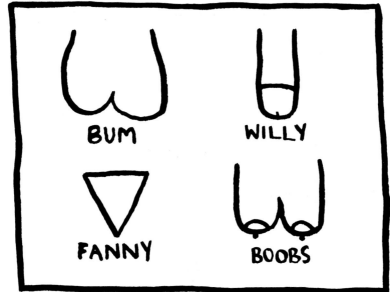

Let us not SNIGGER or be ASHAMED.

Rather let us celebrate the BEAUTY of their SIMPLE PERFECTION.

<u>My Darling</u>

I LOVE you so much
that EVERYTHING
I look at makes me
think of YOU

I WILL LOVE YOU...

Till the oceans run dry
Till the sea meets the sky
Till the fish learn to fly
Through a giant meat pie

INSIGNIFICANT MOMENTS when I have LOVED you with ALL my HEART

The BISCUIT and the POTATO

Neither knew its TRUE SELF
until they found each other

I Love, Respect, Cherish and Admire you for being the FREE and BEAUTIFUL and WONDERFUL Human Being that you are*

*except for when you're being
<u>REALLY</u> <u>ANNOYING</u>

LOVE MONKEY

FEEL his Lovely Love
surround you, for LOVE
is rare and precious - let
us TREASURE it all
we can

THE END